Zerbo Health Remover

and other childhood reminiscences

W. L. Lyons III

ZERBO HEALTH REMOVER
AND OTHER CHILDHOOD REMINISCENCES

iUniverse books may be ordered through booksellers or by contacting:

iUniverse
1663 Liberty Drive
Bloomington, IN 47403
www.iuniverse.com
1-800-Authors (1-800-288-4677)

Because of the dynamic nature of the Internet, any web addresses or links contained in this book may have changed since publication and may no longer be valid. The views expressed in this work are solely those of the author and do not necessarily reflect the views of the publisher, and the publisher hereby disclaims any responsibility for them.

ISBN: 978-1-4917-7995-8 (sc)
ISBN: 978-1-4917-8641-3 (e)

Library of Congress Control Number: 2016902455

Print information available on the last page.

iUniverse rev. date: 3/21/2016

Books by W. L. Lyons III

Wyatt's Obsession
Liza's Gift
Zerbo Health Remover

This book is dedicated to all those infants and yet-to-be born whose childhood lies ahead. Light a firecracker in your mind, and have fun!

Contents

Preface

It isn't the same. After decades of adulthood, I'm positive it will never happen again. It didn't for my children, the neighbors' kids or my friends' kids either. I knew long ago, but simply couldn't give up, and in the end, threw in the towel and acknowledged:

My childhood was unique.

Everyone says that, but I'm certain. It frustrates me that my children didn't soar through their young years the way I did. Then again, I'm sure all parents claim that too.

But it's true.

This understanding has fathered a vague inner madness that compelled me to write these anecdotes about my youth. The chronology may be ragged, and perhaps the facts will be embellished by translucent recollections of a seasoned adult grasping for past glories. But the antics of childhood are old people's memories. So, I write for the joy of remembrance, but more importantly, I hope that everyone will read and come to love my fledgling conquests. In a way, they reflect everyone's youth.

It's important to recognize that in most ways I didn't create my early days, but reacted to those around me. The puppeteers of my early life were my parents, my aunt known as Tante, my brother and sister, David and his parents, Patty (the first girl in my life) and the high school crowd—Jim, Karl, and Larry. I owe them. A lot.

This little book would have been impossible without the incredible help of my wife, Darleen; she's a gem. I'd also like to thank my writers group, particularly Toni Floyd, John McKenzie, and Tom Tucker for thoughtful comments.

Patty &
THE TREE

Shrines.

Kids, in their innocence, marvel at the ordinary. The ordinary is a façade donned by adults to proclaim their sophistication, but in truth, life is always awesome. Kids are right; the world is fresh and new. It's the adults who grow old and stale. If big people were to take a moment from their work and obligations to recall their youth, I bet they'd find a shrine or two. If they're lucky, they might stumble upon a huge golden temple erected by bursts of child insight.

I have such a place. A girl and a tree. Or maybe it's a tree and a girl. As a pre-pubescent boy, they weren't much different. Yet they were, and as I close my eyes, I see it a bit more clearly: a girl *in* a tree. The girl is Patty; the tree is gone.

I last saw Patty when she was in her teens and simply cannot accept the notion that she's become a senior citizen like me. Actually, I can't remember her as a teenager, because at that age I was so frightened of girls that I immersed myself in science, rejecting the ladies in stark terror. I'm unable to conjure her in my memory as a young woman with breasts and a silly giggle.

But somehow, she made me see another person—in spite of the fact that young boys and girls cultivate a strange fetish—mutual hatred. It's all put on, of course, but it's a fashionable pastime before the roaring hormones throw man and woman together forever. Hence, the girls go their way and shun the boys, who in turn scorn the girls as unworthy. So Patty and I had no use for one another at age nine or ten. None.

A sanctuary requires an altar, and mine was the tree. I don't know what kind it was, but I found it perfectly climbable. Located halfway up the block, its foliage threw a mottled shadow on the sidewalk, and large emerald leaves screened its inner reaches from the stares of passersby. Although it appeared to be rather ordinary from the adult perspective, its branches became a wonder for me. When I needed a refuge to ponder the trials of boyhood, I'd often clamber into its branches, searching for solace.

The first time Patty and I climbed the tree together made no impression, and so I have no recollection of the event. I'm sure we shunned and scorned each other appropriately. As a crack climber, I must have been inspired by her ability to scale the heights—in a dress yet! Perhaps that was the catalyst that drew me to her. Before long, we'd meet daily, cradled in the canopy. Glory! My days became a troika: hoping to find Patty in the tree, rejoicing with Patty in the tree, and the aching memory of the day's encounter. I longed for her. I wanted nothing but to be with her, smell her clean aroma, and watch her hair waltz in the summer breeze. The images of her are as vital to me today as if I had just climbed down to the ground moments ago.

She became my shrine.

Patty was slender. Her skin was baby smooth and fair, although the summer sun cast a bold blush on her cheeks. She had fine, straight teeth, which, at that age, were a little too big for her face. Patty's eyes were blue, but not ice blue, and I think she had a gold streak in one iris, but my daughter has such a mark, so I might be confusing them. Her mother cut Patty's blond hair short, so the glittering wisps fluttered about her face, bringing a magical animation to her smile. Fashion-wise, she didn't dress in tennies and jeans—as is the fashion today—but in plaid dresses and lacy socks that peeked about her delicate ankles. Her laugh was soft and shy, and her hands moved quietly when she talked. Patty had a habit of glancing at the ground from time to time, as if she were afraid to hold your eyes too long. With a shy smile, she listened to my boyish boasting and endured my pompous pronouncements. Like butterflies dancing in the sun, we blended and linked that summer. But then, after awhile, new adventures beckoned, and our trysts in the aerie became less frequent. In time, we stopped meeting altogether and went on to other things, the way kids do.

Today, years later, I remember glancing fondly at her parents' house when I drove to my folks' place for a visit. The tree had vanished, and I was bothered that I didn't remember where it stood; it was like losing Westminster Abbey.

Patty and the tree are gemstones in my life. I've set them in the gold statuary of my past, and they glitter like a beacon. The memory has become a shrine to honor a fine person, a sweet moment in time and passage to now. My days in adulthood seem gray and blurred—like rain slithering down a window. Yet Patty beckons from the past, and I nod in homage to her. There have been other temples in my life—one or two—but none so warm as this.

Cherish your shrines.

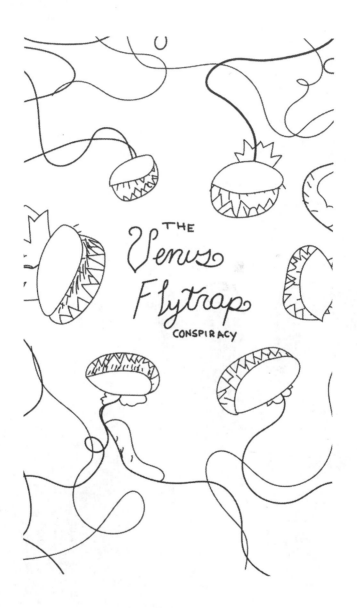

THE

Venus

Flytrap

CONSPIRACY

Anyone who's been around children knows that kids have a mean streak, as assuredly as they have feet. All parents watch their progeny squabble over trivia and mutter, "They'll outgrow it. Just a phase." But in the case of boys, I wonder if it's true.

I was fifteen, an age when I was spellbound by the world of science. As adolescents do, I joined a clique of like-minded guys, and we'd gather in the schoolyard to pontificate on matters of robots, ray guns, and space travel.

Reinforcing the view that males are bred to dominate, our discussions often became heated. Soon, a hierarchy appeared where Jim, Bob, and I ganged up on Larry, whom we'd secretly dubbed "Gullible Gus." Be assured—Larry wasn't halfway gullible; he was world-class gullible.

And we pounced.

I'm not sure where the idea germinated, but we embraced a scheme that involved a fictitious Venus flytrap. It went something like this:

"How ya hanging, Larry?"

"Great. You finish the book report for old lady Hass' class?"

"Naw. I'm too busy with my new pet. A Venus flytrap."

"A *what?*"

"You know. A carnivorous plant. Eats flies."

The puzzled look on Larry's face was gratifying. Either I had stumped him with my newfound big word—*carnivorous*—or he hadn't heard of the plant. So I jammed my thumbs into my belt and puffed out my chest. "I'm growing Igor—I named him Igor—in a special blend of liquid nutrients. Hydroponic agriculture." (More big words.)

"Yeah? What kind?" Larry asked.

"Oh, special plant food from the nursery. Igor has taken a fancy to Seven-Up. Other stuff, too. I'll keep experimenting."

The bell rang announcing the end of lunch period, and Larry, entranced, departed with a slack jaw and a glassy stare. Gullible Gus was hooked, and I strolled to my math class sporting a wide grin.

As school let out later that day, I cornered Jim and Bob to solidify our conspiracy. Guffaws and giggles gave way to roaring laughter as we laid out plans for our hoax.

Two days later, Larry joined Bob and me before civics class. "How's Igor doin'?" he asked.

"He's growing faster than a weed," I said, pleased with my wit.

"Sure is," Bob confirmed with a knowing nod. "We're having trouble catching enough flies. Igor's appetite is taking off like a V-2 rocket."

Larry leapt at the bait. "I can catch some and bring them to school in a jar." His eyes glistened with zeal.

"Great idea!" I affirmed.

So it came to pass. On most mornings, Larry, with a proud grin, presented a jar containing two or three frantic flies.

After a week or so of boasting about Igor's growth, Jim announced, "Guess what, Larry? We added a jigger of bourbon to the hydroponic brew and he shot up to four feet tall. Forget the flies; we can't catch enough. We switched to hamburger meat."

"Yeah," I added. "I can almost see Igor smile at feeding time." I struggled to maintain a solemn look while squelching the mirth raging in my stomach.

"Say, guys," Larry bubbled, "I want to see Igor for myself. How about after school today?"

As accomplished conspirators always are, we were prepared.

"Can't, Larry. Swim practice."

"Me neither. Gotta mow the lawn."

"Need time to study for a test tomorrow. Sorry."

Larry's continued insistence on seeing Igor

ramped up our fictitious weed's growth—and our excuses. Over the next few days, we confided to Larry that we'd added spinach juice to the mixture. As Popeye might, Igor sprang to six feet in height and then eight. His daily diet vaulted from two tablespoons of raw hamburger to three cups. We explained that Igor didn't even notice flies anymore.

At last, Larry became emphatic. "Come on, guys, I *gotta* see Igor."

Jim, Bob, and I covertly nodded to one another. Time for the *coup de grâce*.

"You know, I'm free tomorrow afternoon," I said.

"Me too," harmonized Jim and Bob. "You'll be amazed!"

Larry did a brisk dance of excitement. "Yeah! I'll be there."

The next morning, Larry found us at a lunch table in the quad. As he strolled up, we painted our faces with agony.

"What's the matter, guys? Flunk history?" Larry asked.

Jim, our designated hitter, shook his head. "Nope. Much bigger catastrophe. Igor is gone."

"What?" Larry whimpered.

Bob crossed his arms and donned the expression of a somber mortician. "Tell him what happened, Jim."

Jim cleared his throat and rubbed his eye (to make it water, I suspected). "While we were at school yesterday, Igor ate the neighbor's cat." With a flair for the dramatic, Jim drew a finger across his gullet. "A tuft of fur was all we found."

I shrugged. "That's it, Larry. The neighbor was furious and threatened to call the cops. 'There are small kids on the street!' he yelled. 'Are they next?'"

We lowered our chins to our chests. "Igor's chopped to pieces."

"Dang, fellas. I wanted to feed him," Larry moaned. He jammed his hands into his pockets and, with disappointment glazing his eyes, stumbled off.

As he disappeared, the three of us joyously slugged each other on the shoulder, the rage of the time. When the bell interrupted our celebrations, we strutted to our first class, smug in our superiority.

Had my mother known, she would have said that was a mean stunt. Now that I look back, I'd have to agree.

THE SHACK

Dick, David's father, beat the shit out of him. Constantly. I didn't know that until I was elderly, maybe thirty. Dick was also an alcoholic and so cantankerous that he moved out of his own house and lived in his printing shop that crouched in the backyard. He swore with such venom that it took my breath away. And he read Shakespeare, listened to Mozart, and built the shack for Dave. And me too.

Dave had two backyards: the good backyard with grass, and the back-backyard, which, in a manner of speaking, was bald. The ground was dusty, covered with fine flour-like silt, and forlorn weeds trampled by scurrying young feet. No matter, it was ours. Because the back-backyard couldn't be seen from the house, we could do anything we wished with it. We'd dig World War I trenches and grow corn so high we couldn't see over it. Sometimes we'd flood shallow grooves with the garden hose to recreate the Mississippi River or abuse the ground in a variety of other ways. But, most importantly, the back—backyard harbored the shack.

As a printer, Dick bought paper in large quantities delivered in large wooden crates. Also a woodworker, he decided to build a shack for his son from scrap wood (to amend for the beatings?). I'm not sure how old we were—maybe eight or nine—but from our child-perspective, the shack was immense. It was six by six by six feet high at its lowest point. It had a peaked weatherproof roof and a real door but no glass in the windows. The floor was dirt, but that didn't matter. It became home, the classic tree house of little kids, but this one was on the ground.

A few years later, Dick built an addition, doubling the shack's size. He also put in a wooden floor. Dave and I hung shutters on the windows and padlocked the door to secure our goodies. Somewhere in time, a small concrete porch appeared, probably of leftover concrete from another, more serious adult job. Inside, a rusty, wood-burning pot-bellied stove squatted in the corner. I have no idea where it came from or where it rests now. It was an altar upon which we sacrificed marshmallows, hot dogs, and cans of beans. Our furnishings included a treasure chest, a small roll-top desk, and several crates serving as chaise lounges, tables, and shelves. Dave and I stored Indian spears, sailing ship masts, and freight train rails in the rafters. We hung assorted gardening implements from finishing nails driven into the walls. All in all, the shack was a very serviceable structure.

But it was much more than that. Dave and I often snatched a weed stalk, slipped it between our teeth, and escaped the hot summer sun inside the shack. There, we'd talk about the latest chicken diseases or plot revenge against Fritz, our archenemy. Sometimes Dick melted scrap lead printer's type and poured crude "pirate" coins. Then we'd spread the weighty disks on a crate and count and fondle them, chortling in our wealth. If winter winds flailed rain against the shutters, we'd crouch beside the torrid stove and feel smug in our supremacy over the storm gods.

At other times, a late night candle glow might cast terrifying shadows on the walls. In the flickering light, one of us lifted a well-thumbed copy of Holling C. Holling's *The Book of Indians* from the shelf. Using its illustrations as a guide, we'd whittle Apache war clubs or adorn home-crafted Iroquois bows with feathers. I had *The Book of Cowboys* too, which propelled us into the world of Texas longhorns and ranching. We'd strap on six-shooter cap pistols and try to hog-tie a doggie (Dave's puppy). These books became our sacred texts, bathed in the flickering candlelight just like in a church.

Today, I get immense pleasure when I go to my bookcase and slip these two books from the shelf. Even now, old memories of kid-ventures vault from their pages as I browse through the smudged and tattered pages.

Sometimes we converted the shack into a factory where Dave and I manufactured corncob pipes and walnut shell sailing ships to sell to the neighbors. The two of us cast plaster broaches in spoons which we hawked door-to-door. If the neighbors tired of our chronic peddling, a few never showed it. With patient-looking smiles, they'd swoon over the elegance of our offerings, dig into their pockets for loose change, and buy an item or two. Today, as an adult, I'm certain they chucked our *objects d'art* the moment we turned our backs.

Dave, being older and more organized, kept a diary of our endeavors and a ledger of accounts. The diary's entries tended to be sporadic, but we treated the ledger—black and official looking—with reverence. It listed the bottles we salvaged from the neighborhood's trash, the number of corncob pipes we sold, how many chickens in our flock, and so forth. I'd guess that Dave still has it; I'll have to ask.

Besides serving as corporate headquarters for

our business ventures, the shack became other things. It might be the jailhouse in Tombstone Arizona, a flight operations base in France during the First World War, a Spanish galleon, or perhaps the Matterhorn. Sometimes the transition from mere shack to a saloon, for example, occured with a lightening-stroke of a kid's thought. But to become a Spanish galleon required a pint of rollicking kid-imagination and a gallon of elbow grease.

We erected a mast—actually a long board tied to the side of the shack—and hung a blanket for our sail (until it blew away). We'd prop a ladder against the eave so the galleon's crew (us) could clamor "topside" onto the roof. There I'd squint through a cardboard mailing tube "spy-glass" looking for booty. Dave and I would play "Spanish galleon" for a week or so and add artifacts as we went along, such as treasure chests, eye patches, and wooden swords. Then all at once we decided that "Calvary" was better. The tops'l and mast toppled, the treasure chest became the Wells Fargo strong box, and we nailed a Crayola'd sign above the door proclaiming *Headquarters, 5*th *Calvary, South Dakota Territories.*

Although the shack assumed many roles, often fleeting, it was most often the general store. I suppose that's because the two of us most often favored cowboy lore. But a general store normally resides in a community. So Dave and I built a sprawling town to embrace the shack. Between swigs of Gallo Muscatel, Dick printed, and discarded wood from the paper crates. They say one man's trash is another's treasure. That must be doubly true for kids, because when Dick threw out the empty jugs and stout boards, we salvaged them and created a chicken empire and a magnificent ghost town.

But that's another story or two.

TOMBSTONE

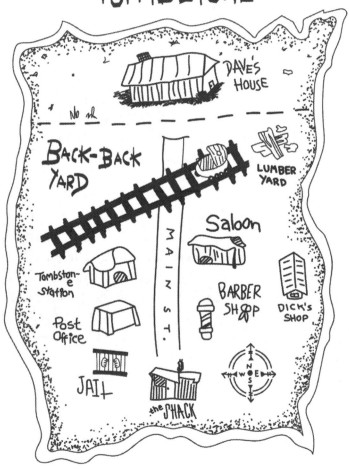

In the fifties, every young boy who shunned western lore lived on Jupiter. But in Downey, California, Dave and I were serious cowboys, replete with cap pistols slung from both hips, ten-gallon hats resting on our ears, and Winchester rifles carved from scrap wood. We'd strut with our thumbs hooked in our belts and spit massive blobs of bubblegum "tobacco" juice on the ground. Lassos and campfires became a religious fervor, and our bible was Holling C. Holling's *Book of Cowboys*. I'm sure that ghosts of past *vaqueros* noted our serious posturing and smiled.

Everyone knows that all cowpokes warm their hands at a pot-bellied stove in the general store. The shack often assumed various roles, but its native state was a general store. Even as youngsters, we knew the shack belonged in the center of a bustling community. A quick glance confirmed that only dirt and weeds surrounded the place, so Dave and I built a sprawling town.

Our first step was to erect a sign over the door of the shack. We salvaged a large piece of lumber and painted bold black letters proclaiming:

TOMBSTONE GENERAL STORE.

The town had its anchor tenant.

With weed stalks clamped between our lips, Dave and I squatted on our hams and drew plans for civic greatness in the dust. We decided the first addition to the town had to be the railroad station. After all, trains hauled lumber, beer, and other key supplies needed by a burgeoning settlement. The new building wasn't much: four feet square by three feet high, but it had a nice sign: **TOMBSTONE STATION.**

Any fool knows a normal station sits alongside train tracks, so Dave and I staked parallel rows of boards diagonally across Main Street, reaching thirty yards toward the house. For rolling stock, we commandeered a discarded baby buggy to serve as a steam locomotive and gondola car. We'd heap boxes of nails, a Wells Fargo strong box (an old wooden crate), and occasionally a wolf (Dave's dog) into the buggy. We'd race down the tracks, hooting our best imitation of a train whistle, the wolf howling harmony.

With transportation assured, we collected boards that Dave's father discarded and stacked them to create a lumberyard at the terminus of the track. A lumberyard, I decided, didn't need a building, so we painted another sign and hammered it into the ground. **LUMBER—CHEAP.**

We studied *The Book of Cowboys*, mulled over the many western movies we'd seen, and realized every town has a post office and a saloon. Unable to decide which to build first, Dave flipped a coin and the post office won. We thrust two-by-four posts into the ground and scabbed on roughly-hewn pine boards to make sides and a leaky roof. It was small—too small to wiggle inside, but there was a window resembling a teller's cage. Dave and I pilfered junk mail from our parents, dropped it in the locomotive (buggy), and roared into town. We'd jam the mail through the window right below the new sign: **TOMBSTONE POST OFFICE.** Very official.

The saloon was bigger—tall enough to stand if we stooped a little. Inside, sturdy shelves held Dave's father's empty gallon wine bottles, and a beat-up coffee can served as a spittoon. Of course, there was another sign. The saloon lacked the usual swinging doors, because serviceable hinges eluded us—a vexing problem for a minute or two until we forgot all about it.

In time, the town jail sprang up and a barbershop. More signs. Both structures were tiny because our interest in construction had begun to wane. Even so, Main Street—boasting six sturdy buildings (not counting the lumberyard)—became a regal, if dusty thoroughfare with the shack presiding over one end and the saloon standing proud at the other.

After school, we'd often shun the weary task of homework. On those days, Dave would howl a vibrant imitation of a wolf to summon me to stride the streets of Tombstone (our backyards abutted). We'd strap on our cap pistols, swagger in the dust, and conjure bold cowboy adventures. Maybe we'd kidnap one of Dave's sister's dolls and toss it in the jail. Other times we'd swill Coke as we hunched over in the saloon. There were times when we...

The town served us well for several years, even during those times when Dave and I played Army, Indians or Pirates. True to tradition, we inevitably returned to playing Cowboys, and Tombstone was there to greet us.

Boys have another tradition: they grow up. Sometime between junior high and high school, we abandoned the town. Dave went his way and I mine. The wooden tracks rotted, and the signs became sun-bleached and toppled in the wind. Our little buildings, tossed together by small impatient hands, disintegrated into piles of gray boards and rusty nails. The shack, being much larger and built by Dave's father, survived many years—only to be demolished along with the main house to make way for a new apartment building.

Today, many decades later, I wish I could stride into the shack on a blustery afternoon, light a fire in the cast-iron stove, and plan a few adventures with buddy Dave. I wish I could find the locomotive and the paintbrush stiff with hardened enamel. I wish...

No matter! Whenever I close my eyes, Tombstone leaps to life. I walk down Main Street, shove a stack of mail into the maw of the post office, and spit another juicy missile at the Folgers spittoon. The weight of pistols hangs heavy at my side, and I smell the dryness of the dust. There are prints of tennis shoes in front of the barbershop, and I can hear Dave grunt as he swings a hammer. I revel in the joy of building a burgeoning village and feel the pride that oozed from each board and nail.

If asked, many adults I know today might think back and say, "The highlight of my life? Well, I once broke a hundred at golf."

Me? I built a town.

FARM

One of the first undertakings of ancient societies was agriculture. It seems right that if civilization sprang to life in a garden, so should the lives of young boys.

On one of those sparkling spring days—when adventurism dispelled any thought of homework—fate mandated that Dave and I become farmers. After sauntering into our shack and hunkering on lettuce crates commandeered from the grocery store, we discussed ways to spend the morning. Ideas flew like a swarm of hornets.

"How about Little Army?"

"Naw. Let's rig the shack as a ship and play Pirates."

"Can't. We used the mast to build the hitching post in our ghost town."

Unable to agree, a cloud of silence seeped into the air. But idleness is not in boys' genes, so the God of Kids mysteriously intervened and tugged our eyes to the corner of the shack where a shovel languished.

Somehow, our minds synchronized. *Shovel. Digging. Digging what?*

Seconds stretched into minutes.

"Let's plant corn," I blurted, recalling a photo of Iowa farmland in my mother's travel magazine.

Dave squinted and crossed his arms. "Just corn?"

I shrugged. "Maybe radishes too?"

"Need seeds. The nursery sells all kinds."

"Got any money?"

We dug in our pockets, rummaged through our bedroom drawers, and managed to pool $1.57. Within moments, Dave and I jumped on our bikes and raced to the store, just minutes away. (Downey was a small town back then.)

Soon, we retreated to the shack clutching assorted seed packets.

Dave studied the planting directions on the back of an envelope. "Four inches apart. Water regularly. Mulch.

Fertilize. Spray for pests," he read. "Any idea what this stuff means?"

"Greek to me," I admitted. "Wasn't your mom raised on a farm? Maybe we could ask her."

The idea of ten-year-olds consulting an adult was as foreign to us as Bulgaria, but helplessness rests uneasy on boys' egos. (The age when we knew *everything* was still two or three years away.) So, with humble, downcast eyes, we visited the oracle—Dave's mother.

Later, fortified with wisdom, we dug a large plot in the back-backyard where parents never ventured. Dave and I took turns on the shovel while the other separated weeds from clods. As the sun set, we stood shoulder to sore shoulder and admired the bounty of the day's work— furrows, only a little crooked, the same as a real farm.

The next morning, a Sunday, Dave and I planted squash, scallions, corn, and radishes. After a thorough watering, we stood and waited for the first sprouts. After twenty minutes, nothing had happened, so I decided to reread the seed packets.

"Says it takes four weeks before radishes are ready. Corn and squash are worse. Gotta wait at least two months."

Dave, a year older than I, decided he was old enough to pilfer his dad's colorful vocabulary. "Crap," he grumbled. Antsy for action, the fledgling farmers abandoned the plot and played Cowboy the rest of the day.

Dave and I returned the next afternoon and decided hand watering was too laborious. We devised a primitive irrigation scheme by leveling the furrows and building earthen dams to channel water from the hose.

Unlike most of our endeavors, Dave and I became very diligent about this undertaking. Every day after school, we'd water, yank weeds, and strut along the rows like weatherworn farmers. The farm lacked money for fertilizer and pesticides, and our parents ignored pleas for more money. Hence, Dave and I added a new routine to our daily chores—picking bugs and snails from the stalks by hand. We considered gathering dog turds from the neighborhood for fertilizer, but decided there were too many plants and too few dogs. When green sprouts finally thrust themselves from the earth, we slipped foxtail stalks between our teeth and gloated in our skills.

Finally, the farm yielded its first crop—a handful of radishes! We went to the shack and crunched the fruits of our labors, so to speak. We boasted that they were definitely the finest ever grown and talked about going to the local Safeway grocery to see if they'd buy a few bunches. The idea died, simply because we ate them all.

Autumn revealed a bountiful stand of corn and sprawling squash plants. We'd replanted the scallions and radishes, and the new crop burst through the warm soil. Both our parents welcomed the boy-grown veggies and served them nightly, slathered with real butter and salt (try that today.) An unintended consequence: unlike most kids (or adults for that matter), I still enjoy vegetables.

Today, decades later, I realize we had created the first organic farm ever, if you discount the efforts of emerging hunter-gatherers. Dave and I were trendsetters back then; we just didn't know it.

The farm continued for several years and expanded into the chicken business as well. Corncobs from the dinner table ended up in the chicken coops, where the birds picked them clean. When dry, we transformed them into corncob pipes that we hawked door-to-door to the neighbors.

Chickens and pipes you ask? Well, that's another tale or two.

the
CHICKEN BUSINESS

Dave and I were twelve or so when we decided chickens were the wave of the future. It was one of those mellow Southern California afternoons when we couldn't decide what to do. We squatted in Dave's backyard and indulged in our surefire "Let's get something goin' routine" by alternately suggesting exciting endeavors.

"Catch tadpoles?" Dave uttered.

I scowled. "Badminton?"

"Feed moths to the spiders?" Dave was in his "Great White Hunter" mood that day.

"Indians?"

"Ride our bikes to the donut shop?"

Our imagination exhausted, a silence settled

over us like the fine silt that covered the backyard. Lost in thought, I wielded a twig similar to a fencer's foil, tracing geometric patterns in the dust. Dave exhumed a rock from the ground and turned it over and over, studying every crevice as the stone tumbled in his palm. The seconds slowly plucked themselves from the realm of the future and eased into history.

"Chickens," Dave murmured.

"What?"

"Chickens. Let's raise chicks and sell eggs to the neighbors. We'll be rich!"

"How long does it take before a chicken starts laying eggs?" I asked.

"Around six months, I'm guessing," Dave said.

"Sheee-it! That's forever!"

He stood, uncoiled his skinny frame, and flung the rock into a nearby shrub. "Billy, the egg business is a good business." (He always spoke of such matters as if he'd been doing it for years.) "But we're nearly broke. The butchering age for fryers is less, much less. No more than three months. Maybe we could butcher half to get quick money and then raise the other half for eggs."

Like a candle's glimmer on a moonless night, the idea began to penetrate my reluctant mind. Chickens—kinda like ranching. I stood, spun on my heel, and took several exaggerated steps to see if strutting like a rancher felt good. It did. I jammed my hands deep into the pockets of my jeans to see if slouching like a rancher felt good. It did. Visions of vast flocks swirled in my head, and the thunder of endless clucking throats assailed my ears. "How many?" I asked.

"Huh?" blurted Dave, jarred from his own reveries.

"How many chickens?"

"Oh, hundreds—*thousands!*"

Thus it came to pass; we embraced the chicken business. Dave and I never had thousands, but hundreds became a reality. Not right away, of course. After pooling our meager resources and pedaling our bikes to the feed store, we found we could afford twenty chicks (fifteen cents apiece) and ten pounds of feed. With boundless pride, we gently cradled a box of yellow fuzz-balls in our arms as we rode twelve blocks back to "The Ranch." We were unaware that our suburb was zoned R-1 (no chickens). Our parents grimaced at the sight, and my mother muttered, "Another phase." Dave's parents lost. We set up ranching in his backyard, not mine.

That night I crawled into my cool bed, and in the zeal of youth I saw a limitless future as a rancher. As I slipped into his domain, the Sandman smiled and blessed me with rousing dreams of bold chicken adventures.

Dave and I soon learned our chicks had voracious appetites, so we funded our feed bin by rummaging through the neighbors' trashcans salvaging bottles. We redeemed them for a nickel apiece at the Downey paint store. Soon after embarking on this side business, I overheard my father say to a friend, "Oh, those kids who grub around in trash cans? Nope. Don't know them."

Unlike most of our childhood adventures, we persisted with the ranch. Dave and I salvaged scrap lumber, built a coop for the younger birds, and fenced in a large area for the older ones. We soon expanded and moved our butchering operations into my father's lath house. Overgrown with ivy, it was dank but had two useful features: gas burners and a concrete table tucked into the rambling foliage. We rolled a huge pepper tree log in front of the stove, turned it on its end, and drove two large nails side by side to resemble closely spaced goal posts. This served to stretch the chicken's necks while we dispatched them to fryer heaven with a machete.

The first bird was a true test of our manliness; I suspect Dave wanted to vomit as much as I did when he severed the first head. The bird gushed enough blood to float a small dingy. Dave was so startled that he let go of the chicken which flew off like a headless condor. Over time, however, we became suitably calloused.

We'd boil a large pot of water on the burner, dunk the lifeless birds so we could pluck their feathers, and then dress them out on the concrete table. Dave's mother instructed us on avian anatomy, and today I can still cut up a fryer in record time.

Our marketing efforts were crude. With soulful faces, we'd go door-to-door in the neighborhood offering chickens, drawn or dismembered, guaranteed fresh. Some customers, such as the wealthy Mrs. Burridge next door, would insist on selecting her evening meal while it was on the hoof—in this case, on its last legs. Two hours later, we'd deliver her dinner with thumbs hooked in our belt loops just like real ranchers.

Flush with cash and reliable customers, we forsook eggs altogether. Today's politicians would call us flip-floppers, but I think of it more in terms of a mid-course correction.

Many months later, after purchasing another batch of fifty chicks (maybe a hundred, I don't remember), we pedaled home pelted by a drenching rain. Lacking a waterproof shelter for the fragile chicks, Dave and I decided to house them in the kneehole of my built-in bedroom desk. We spread newspapers, put in a desk lamp for warmth, and enclosed the entire proceedings with the fireplace screen we had snatched from the living room. Later that night, my parents came home from shopping and took one glance at the rapidly accumulating droppings covering the newspaper. They slapped their foreheads and settled into industrial-strength martinis.

That night, my mother went into labor with my sister.

The chicks survived their ordeal, and we ushered them into their normal coop the next morning.

The beginning of the end came on a dark and stormy night (yes, I know it's trite). That's when Dave and I learned about *coccidiosis*, a highly contagious poultry disease, always fatal. Our entire flock was wiped out. It was a hard lesson of life. We dug a pit in Dave's backyard and tossed the carcasses, layered by lime, into the hole. With arms crossed, we stood silently and pondered our future as non-ranchers. I don't know about Dave, but that was when I began to doubt God's existence.

But kids are resilient. Dave pursued his entrepreneurial bent by taking a newspaper route, and I followed suit. Even though the paper was a throwaway, it led me to discover a hidden side of my persona. But that's another tale.

Bicycle Vagabonds

When someone says that boys have an appendage that girls don't, they usually aren't talking about what I, as a little kid, visualized: a bicycle. My parents didn't get me a bike until I could manage a full-size model, so I consider myself an abused child. No matter! From around age eight or nine and extending through my freshman year in college, I was biologically joined to the handlebar of my bike—a true appendage.

My bicycle appeared under the tree at dawn on a rainy Christmas morning—a stunning new J. C. Higgins. My mechanical bent, which blossomed into a career years later, provided the solution to my father's dictum: "No, you can't ride outside. It's raining. Not inside either!" So, I grabbed a wrench and removed both wheels and the pedals just to see how they were attached. Mother had a conniption fit, but I suspect my father, an engineer, was secretly pleased.

As always in Southern California, the weather cleared, and the afternoon saw flocks of youngsters on their new bikes, scooters, and wagons flitting along sidewalks and barreling down the street. After reassembling my treasure, I learned my first trick. I'd careen along the sidewalk to my house, slam on the brake (coaster-style in those days), and deposit a long black skid-mark on the concrete in front of the porch. This stunt annoyed my father no little. The habit persisted for years.

My new bike had a dual headlight where two adjoining pods housed the bulbs. My imaginative kid brain triggered a vision: the two pods became engine nacelles on a P-38 fighter plane. To bolster the illusion, I clipped playing cards to the fender with clothespins, which sputtered in the spokes, creating the thunder of the fighter's twin Allison V-12s.

When Dave and I became bored with playing "dogfighting German Messerschmitts," our mounts might become dragsters and we'd race on my dead-end street. We'd start our contest at Cherokee Road and blast past Patty's and Screwdie's houses. With competitive zeal, we'd hurtle between two massive posts that marked the end of the street and the entrance into the Tyler family's private enclave. We discovered such antics annoyed some people, because as we pedaled back up the street for another race, Mr. Tyler hooked a heavy cable between the posts. As we blazed down the road again, Dave must have seen the barrier and backed off. I thought I had him for sure and thrust even harder on the pedals. *Wham!* Bike stopped—Billy didn't. I still have a scar on my knee where the speedometer bracket carved out a chunk of boy-meat. The next day, we bombarded the Tyler's garage with oranges from the orchard next door. Never fool with kids.

As I grew older, the bike expanded my horizons; no longer was I confined to my street. On crystal clear winter mornings, the Whittier Hills beckoned as if they were next door; in reality, they were nine miles away. The distance was no match for the fearless energy of youth. In the brisk chill, while our parents still slumbered, Dave and I braved the four-lane treachery of Lakewood Boulevard and pedaled until the sharp grade of the foothills conquered our weary legs. Panting, we'd rejoice in our conquest and race downhill toward home, passing astonished motorists. The speedo on my bike could hit forty if I were earnest!

Pumping a bike eighteen miles has an obvious effect on kids: hunger. We had a favorite donut shop where I often devoured three maple bars and guzzled a cup of coffee. Because both my parents drank coffee, I marked it as a sign of adulthood—important to a kid. Even now I drink a pot a day.

As in many small eateries of that era, the donut shop had a jukebox where you could pick out four songs for a quarter. We'd strut to the machine like big shots and pick out a few tunes. One in particular was *awful*; it was called *Truck Drivin' Man*. The first time we played it, we shuddered over the twangy guitar and silly lyrics, and vowed never to play it again.

But we did. One morning, the feisty demons

that lurk in young boys' minds took command of our senses. Dave and I dug into the pockets of our jeans, pooled five quarters for the jukebox, and punched in *Truck Drivin' Man twenty times*. Laughing hilariously, we ran to our bikes and fled, imagining shrieks of agony gushing from the proprietor. Other patrons, I'm sure, abandoned half-eaten donuts after two or three repetitions. I heard *Truck Drivin' Man* on the radio a few days ago. I had to smile.

The last bicycle hurrah came when I was a freshman in junior college. Three professed engineering majors (including me) struck out from Long Beach for Las Vegas over Easter break. Two of us made it; the third gave up after only a few blocks. After three sweaty days, we arrived in Vegas smelling like wet dogs, and pedaled over to Hoover dam, where we rode the elevator down to see the generators. My friend and I stood in the middle of the car while the other riders shrank against the walls, beat back, I suspect, by our reek. That night, camping in a culvert, my buddy snickered that the scene resembled germs being repelled by a vaccine.

As I write this, my memory skitters from one adventure to another. Like when Dave and I would tie wagons to our bikes and haul discarded bottles to the paint store for money to buy feed for our chickens. Or when I'd sling a canvas bag of newspapers across the bike's handlebars and struggle along my paper route.

But those are other tales.

Poetry in the Fog

Poetry stands as an essence of youth, an integral part of a mind unfettered by the mental calluses called experience. I can't recall anyone who hasn't tried poetry as a kid and know of no adults who still write poetry. I think most wish they did, and count the loss as a measure of their advancing years. Poetry is something special; kids are special, and thus they belong to one another.

I can't remember if I was in junior high or in the early years of high school when disease ravished our chicken business. Dave, needing an outlet, got a paper route. He delivered a local throwaway called *The Herald American*. I was livid with jealousy, so I got a route too. As it turned out, the job was a pain in the ass, simply because I was allergic to early morning.

It lasted only a few months until I gave up on dark mornings and trying to collect "voluntary" fees for a rag nobody wanted—a rather unique feature of the *Herald American*.

In the middle of the night while I slumbered, a truck—it must have been a truck, although I never saw it—dumped a huge bundle of newspapers between the two palm trees that stood like sentinels in our front yard. At four in the morning or thereabouts, I'd stagger into the damp darkness to fold each paper, wrap them with rubber bands, and stuff them into a grubby canvas bag. How I hated it! It was cold as only California can be. While the thermometer might register temperate temperatures, the dank sea air burrowed through my jacket and flannel shirt as if they were gossamer.

But something happened on those gray foggy mornings when the mist hung in the air and cradled the early hours in its quiet fold. The streetlight across the road by my friend Screwdie's house formed a gentle halo that bathed the palms in a soft glow and made the dew-laden grass glisten. It was always quiet, quiet as a cat's breathing. Perhaps a distant truck purred briefly but never loud enough to intrude. While I squatted on the grass, the palms, halo, and paper bundle seemed to recede from reality as kid-imagination burst forth, hurling sparkling visions against the gloom.

Detached hands slapped each newspaper into thirds and whipped resentful rubber bands around the fold's girth, but the boy took no notice. The hands turned black from raw printer's ink as they jammed paper after paper into the canvas, but the boy's mind sailed through the drifting fog into the ether beyond. Love, glory, and song peeked between the thrashing pages, and heroes dashed about their business. Somehow, a clean bit of paper appeared, the stained fingers produced a stubby pencil, and the boy forgot about the *Herald American*.

He wrote poetry, noble poetry. A torrent of words spewed from the tooth-pocked pencil. The boy sat cross-legged on the grass with his nose close to the paper, so he could see in the gloom. Dew crept through his pants, making his legs and butt shiver with the chill—but the poetry flowed uninterrupted.

Fog collected on the leaves, ran in little slow motion rivulets to their tips, and then spattered to earth. Slinking through time, dawn turned the blackness to milk. The streetlight's halo faded and slipped into the realm of history. A bird, bolder than most, chirped his greeting to the pending dawn.

The boy jolted. *Late!* The paper and pencil were stuffed into a pocket, and the blackened hands— my hands—thrust the last of the folded papers into the canvas sack. I heaved and struggled with the bag to sling it across the handlebars of my bike. Lurching on the pedals, I wobbled down the pot-holed road, while the newspapers tried furiously to jam the spokes of the front wheel. A distant truck whined in the thinning fog, and the poetry grinned in my pocket.

Now, looking though my papers, I find a few sheets poetry, mostly of a later era—my college phase. Some had its roots, I'm sure, in those morning fogs. But sadly, disastrously, no sheets of poetry are smudged by printer's ink.

My Favorite Song

"What's your favorite song?" is a common question, one that seems to command a firm response. Everyone *always* has a favorite song. After a time, so did I.

When I let my mind wander back to grade school, I can recall an animated conversation between several boys regarding their respective taste in music. The presence of a cute girl made the occasion somewhat pontifical. Being rabidly interested in the girl, I joined the group. The guys stood with feet spread and their thumbs hooked in their belt loops (*cool, man, cool*) and argued avidly about one Top 40 hit after another. I was lost, having never listened to music of any kind.

But one does not impress cute girls with profound silence, so at appropriate intervals I inserted, "Well, maybe..." or "Yeah, that's right." The most dominant guy insisted Kay Starr's *Wheel of Fortune* (not to be confused with that sophomoric TV show) was the only song a cool person should listen to. Others disagreed. The debate became more and more heated, so the group confronted the mousy guy (me) to cast the deciding ballot.

"Well?" they demanded. *The Wheel of Fortune* guy made threatening faces and flexed his bountiful biceps. The cute girl giggled. I'm no fool, and *Wheel of Fortune* became my first favorite song. Curious, I rummaged around in the den that night and found the song in my mother's record pile. It was awful.

Sometime in high school I decided it was time to polish my public image and seriously indulge in music. I'd shaved once or twice, and it was time to become a sophisticate. I knew that socially acceptable people danced and bought records (45s in those days—no iPods). One afternoon I stole into a record store and stopped in front of a display of current hits. Two caught my eye: *Oop Shoop* and *Sh-Boom*. Those were very cool names. With a suave smirk, I plunked down my money and scurried home to play them. Both were terrible, but realizing I'd be an outcast if my revulsion became public knowledge, I struggled to overcome my disgust. After weeks of aural agony, I assumed I had a severe genetic defect and gave up music altogether.

By the time I became a senior in high school, I had decided the role of intellectual whiz better suited my skinny physique and rather odd tastes. So I rejected anything "normal." This epiphany, plus a stray comment from my father, introduced me to my first genuine favorite song.

A few days before Christmas, I was in dire need of a gift for my father when I discovered a two-record set of Beethoven. The jacket said something about the First and Ninth, but I was clueless what that meant. I'd never heard a Beethoven piece and had no hope of even spelling it, but it was "good music" (my father's phrase). Regardless, its price matched my resources, so I bought the album and presented it on Christmas morning. I got that polite tight-lipped grin that meant I had blown it. But he thanked me graciously (he was always gracious unless I left my socks on the floor) and even played a side that afternoon. My gift gathered dust for the next two weeks.

I was in the habit of rising early before leaving for school. Often, I'd futz around with model airplanes or torment my brother for more than an hour. One morning, out of kid-style boredom, I played one of the Beethoven records. The "Ninth." Strange as it might seem, it caught my ear. I played it the next morning and again that afternoon after school. I even tried to whistle the tunes. Ever whistle a symphony? A contrapuntal Beethoven symphony? No matter—I whistled it without stopping. In keeping with my new "rebel" image, I embraced Beethoven because he never appeared on the TV program *Hit Parade*, the accepted authority of pop music. I'd brag to my classmates at school how wonderful Beethoven was, and to my delight, they were revolted—most satisfying.

Within six months, I had worn the record out. My father didn't notice. Annoyed with the scratching and popping of his battered disk, I joined a record club and bought another, and another. I even branched out into Mozart, Rachmaninoff and other ancients.

In the ensuing decades, I've listened to the "Ninth" several hundred times, maybe a thousand or two. The third movement is proof there's a heaven, and I've asked that it be played at my funeral—no eulogy please.

I'd guess you'd say the "Ninth" became my favorite song.

As a postscript, I'm forced to admit that somewhere around age forty or forty-five, Beethoven acquired a partner on my shrine of exalted music: Dolly Parton followed by Emmylou Harris. Others shouldered their way alongside Beethoven including Vivaldi, Wagner, and Willie Nelson. Now, when asked what's my favorite song, I'm liable to launch into a virtually interminable discourse. Perhaps I should just say *Wheel of Fortune* and leave them in bewilderment.

Algae Amok

Because I spent my formative years in the fifties, I'm convinced it was a special era. It was the time of Elvis' *All Shook Up*, cars with fins (the iconic '57 Chevy), the birth of McDonald's, and the greatest earth-shaker ever—The Pill. But for me, a self-proclaimed scientific, I was obsessed—not with burgers or sex—but with rockets and space.

During high school lunch or at the donut shop after class, a few of us scientifics would huddle and talk about rockets, launches at White Sands, or visions of future moon colonization. These were not casual encounters, but spiritual gatherings where we venerated Robert Goddard and Werner Von Braun. We held forth on thrust, velocity, and propellant combinations—our Gregorian chant, if you will.

Any fool knows there's no air in space, so future astronauts were condemned to lug around immense tanks of oxygen. As a teenager unburdened by practical experience, I thought that was ridiculous. But what to do?

One bright fall afternoon as I squatted alongside my father's fishpond (no fish, just scum), the Space Travel God revealed himself.

"Look at the scum," He commanded. So I did and shrugged. It was just scum.

"Think," the Holy One commanded.

My thoughts plodded through the halls of chemistry class, biology, and even the many well-worn books I'd collected about space.

Suddenly I had a flash of insight. *Not scum. It's algae. It converts carbon dioxide into oxygen. Exactly what future rocket pilots need!* Shouting and waving my hands, I realized that algae, nourished by sunlight and the spent breath of astronauts, could flourish and bequeath precious oxygen. The Space Travel God smiled and slipped into memory.

As a budding scientific, I formulated a plan to grow algae. Little green bugs from the pond could be harvested, and I'd rig an electric lamp to provide twenty-four-hour sunlight. But a reliable source of carbon dioxide eluded me. I asked my chemistry teacher for advice, and—after cynically grilling me

algae...
carbon
dioxide...
OXYGEN!

about my intentions—he offered the solution: mix marble chips and hydrochloric acid to get carbon dioxide.

I was already on a first name basis with the counter guy at Cenco Scientific where I'd purchased bottles of mercury (try *that* today,) supplies for my chemistry set, and assorted ingredients for rocket fuel. The next day, I was the proud possessor of a gallon jug of acid and a box of marble chips.

The pungent acid attacked my nose, so I decided to set up the experiment in the garage, rather than my room. I asked my father for permission, of course, but he was preoccupied with the newspaper and just nodded. Good enough.

One look at the grubby single-car garage mandated a major remodel. I swept the workbench clear of junk, emptied a sagging shelf, and scrubbed the grime away. I pilfered glassware, stoppers, and tubing from my chemistry set, and in kid-exuberance, assembled a glorious scientific apparatus.

Darkness descended, and the feeble light bulb, high in the rafters, proved inadequate, so I abandoned the project for the night.

Dawn found me in the garage once more, where I tossed the chips into a flask, filled a beaker with fresh pond scum, and started a siphon from the acid bottle perched high on the shelf. *Drip, drip, drip* into the marble. As predicted, the chips bubbled merrily, and the gaseous elixir percolated into my beaker of contented little algae. I snapped on the desk lamp that I'd snatched from my room and, satisfied my elegant experiment was working to perfection, reluctantly left for school.

There, puffed up with pride, I boasted to my fellow scientifics: Larry, Karl, and Jim. The first period bell halted their accolades, and we parted—agreeing to meet after school at my house to check the health of the little green bugs. Anxious, I spent the entire day mentally rehearsing my triumphal victory speech to my friends.

That afternoon, we all rushed to "the laboratory" where a vile odor that I immediately recognized as hydrochloric acid, assailed us. Disaster! The siphon had run amok. Acid had overflowed the algae beaker, eaten into the bench top and had pooled on the concrete floor where it simmered like a witch's caldron. Not only had the algae been killed, but also every piece of metal in the garage had succumbed to the vapors and donned the dull reddish-brown color of rust.

"Is algae supposed to be brown?" asked Larry.

"Only dead ones," Karl said.

Grateful that my father had taken the car to work and thus evaded the rust assault, I clamped off the siphon. Gasping in the toxic air, we hosed the floor and oiled the Crescent wrench, hoe, and myriad other steel objects.

Breathless, I agonized over the vagaries of science and the aggressive nature of acid.

My victory speech receded into the realm of embarrassment and hard knocks.

Karl rubbed his close-cropped flattop. "Nice try, Billy, but it's obvious you're a dangerous scientific. I have a new model airplane engine I plan to test. A jet. If you want a lesson in genuine research, maybe you can lend a hand."

So, a few days later, I joined Karl in *his* garage.

But that's another tale.

KARL AND THE PULSE JET

Karl Mueller seemed as Germanic as his name; he had a crisp manner of speech, a short-clipped flattop, and impeccable clothes. Above all, he was scientific. Not a wimpy, gazing-through-thick-eyeglasses scientific, but a bright, sparkling scientific.

Perhaps we went to grade school or junior high together, but we never knew it, because the time wasn't right. I'd guess it was during the spring of our senior year in high school that our destinies crossed. The moment was brief, but it gave me a lifelong appreciation for persistence.

The catalyst was a piece of pipe.

You see, I was a devout scientific too, and Karl's pipe drew me into his orbit like the then-unknown black hole. It became our mutual passion.

Dynajet was its name, a small jet engine comprised of a tube with a metal reed attached to one end similar to a clarinet. If fledgling scientifics wired a battery to its glow plug, and if they pumped vigorously on a tire pump whose hose was jammed down the tube's throat, and if they dribbled appropriate doses of model airplane fuel into the pipe, and if they set their tongues at proper angles in the mouth—it would light. The uninspiring mechanism became a pulse jet engine with a roar that shattered ears and set dogs to barking for blocks.

During civics class, we drew designs for mounting brackets, and that afternoon we tried to mount the engine on the workbench in Karl's garage. I cannibalized my old erector set (Mother was pissed), and—predicting the pipe might get warm—we used hot pads "found" in Karl's mother's kitchen. It took perhaps a week before we concluded our preparations.

I've never been so nervous as when we gassed the Dynajet the first time. This is an ironic thing when one is reminded that later in life, I made my living testing *real* rocket engines, *big* rocket engines! It lay there, lashed to the bench, looking sinister indeed. Karl swept aside a dozen paint cans and filled the small gas tank while I positioned the tire pump. We'd composed an official-sounding checklist figuring it would be more scientific, and I proceeded to intone the ritual.

"Gas?"

"Filled," Karl replied.

"Pump's ready. Glow plug on?"

Karl clipped on the wires. "Go."

"Here comes the juice," I said, removing the vise grip pliers from the plastic fuel tubing. "Gas dribblin'?"

Karl squinted into the pipe. "Yup. Pump it!"

I lunged like a maniac on the tire pump, blasting wheezy shots of air past the reed into the bowels of the pipe.

"More!" cried Karl.

I panted like an eighty-year-old marathoner as I heaved on the handle, but nothing happened.

"Abort," declared Karl. We sat cross-legged on the cold concrete floor and stared at the defiant device, frustration enveloping us.

"What do you think?"

"Don't know."

Soon we filled the garage with profound scientific utterances. Diagnoses burst forth followed by sketches and—ultimately—action. About a week later, a vastly altered test setup brought life to the Dynajet.

The engine, now inclined at a sharp angle, belched as I gave a superhuman thrust on the pump. Karl and I glanced at one another, his bright, straight teeth flashing. "Again!" he growled.

Adrenaline surged into my bloodstream. "Go bitch," I hissed under my breath.

"*Burp!*" said the engine.

Together, Karl and I chanted, "Go bitch, go bitch, go bitch!" as I hurled myself on the pump handle.

Burp, burrp, burrpppp, roarrrrrr!

Karl and I shrieked, whooped, and slugged each other on the shoulder, the current rage. The engine howled and grew a cherry-red mantle, which promptly set fire to the hot pad. Bright yellow flames leapt from the pipe and licked the legs of the wooden workbench. In our ecstatic celebration, we failed to see the pyrotechnic tendencies of our engine. No matter. A stunning silence filled the garage when the machine ran out of gas, leaving smoldering cloth and charred wood.

We simultaneously understood the gravity of the moment and ceased our childish hollering. With solemn expressions, we faced one another and shook hands in the fog-like smoke.

Scientifics will prevail.

We started the engine a few more times, but once predictability had been established, interest waned. I took no notice of the last time I walked from Karl's garage. I took no notice that we rarely spoke after that. I took no notice that the time for Karl and I had ended.

Years later, at my tenth-year high school reunion, I glanced through the alumni directory listing addresses of classmates. My eyes flickered past Karl's name, and then settled back.

"Karl Mueller," it said. "Deceased."

There in the joyous cacophony of the party, eleven years after chanting "Go bitch" in exquisite harmony with Karl, I wept for him, a fellow scientific.

THE CIGAR

Sibling rivalry is a plague that ravishes any family blessed with two or more kids. Mine was no exception. I could pursue a litany of incidents when my brother and I waged war, but one particular event lingers in my memory. It wasn't a genuine battle, but a bout of one-upmanship.

I cherished the three-year advantage I held over my brother, Mark. In 1958 I was a freshman in junior college, a big-deal academic—he a mere high school wimp. As a mature adult, I drove a car to school; he pedaled a bike. I hung out at the college quad sipping coffee; he swilled milk from small cartons. While I'd outgrown the petty pranks I played on Mark in the early days, I still sought ways to demean the little urchin who'd pestered me for sixteen years.

A special opportunity unfolded at Uncle Gabe's restaurant in Downey, California—a modest eatery where my parents often took us for dinner.

One particular night brought the most memorable quote ever uttered by my mother when the waiter asked, "Madam, would you care for a glass of water?" To which she replied, "Young man, I'm thirsty, not dirty. Bring me a martini." I made a mental note for when I ordered my first martini.

At nineteen, I embraced the trappings of an adult, so I naturally took up smoking like my parents did. I was, after all, a real man. Cigarettes were my normal choice, but when in an expansive mood, a cigar was a better choice.

After an uneventful meal, I bought an after-dinner cigar from the case in the entry (yes, they did that in those days). Back at the table, while my parents sipped their coffee, I licked the cigar the way experienced smokers do and lit up, covertly blowing smoke toward my brother out the side of my mouth. Ah yes—I could feel the hair growing on my chest.

Mark didn't take this sitting down, so he announced, "I want a cigar, too."

My parents, being remarkably liberal, glanced at each other and shrugged.

I saw my opening. "Good idea, Mark. I'll even buy you one."

With a wary look, he accepted my kindness. "Sure."

"One condition," I warned. "You have to smoke it to an inch from the end."

"No problem."

I went back up front and bought the biggest,

blackest, cheapest cigar in the case. With a flourish, I presented it to Mark.

He imitated me and tore off the wrapper, licked the cigar, and drew in deep puffs as I held the match.

I'm a helpful soul.

After a few minutes of bombast, Mark's chitchat tapered off. He glared at his cigar with a critical eye—judging its length, I'd guess. I figured he hoped each drag consumed at least half an inch. With a debonair wave of my own cigar, I offered encouraging banter. Our parents just grinned.

On the way home, I was overjoyed to see Mark gulp, roll open the car window, and suck in an immense lungful of air. Between his desperate gasps, I detected a distinct green hue on his face.

I dwelt in heaven.

Back home, he collapsed on the front porch and held out the cigar. "How long is it?" he wheezed.

Always anxious to lend a hand, I sprang to the garage and snatched a ruler. Back on the porch, I steadied his shaking hand and assured him, "Only two inches to go."

Incapable of forming words, he gurgled and took another puff.

I lounged beside him and cheered every drag. "Just an inch to go."

Great fun.

It was late at night by the time he'd finished the job. Mark staggered like a drunk, so I helped him first to the bathroom where he deposited his dinner and then to bed where he passed out. Because I'd dispatched my own cigar without discomfort, I felt very grownup. Conveniently, I'd forgotten my first bout with a stogy.

After watching TV for a while, I decided to turn in. Like many brothers of that era, Mark and I shared a room. Our beds were parallel with each headboard against a small window. With pleasure, I saw Mark was almost Kelly green, and his breath convulsive. Smug in my superiority, I nodded off and dreamt of serious adult things, such as becoming President.

When I awoke the next morning, the sight of my brother filled me with pure ecstasy. During the night, Mark had opened the window, set his pillow on the sill, and slept with his head outdoors in the clean dew-laden night air. I chuckled. *Children. Serves him right.*

As always, there were unintended consequences.

Dave's House, the Bog

I think most kids today find their parents so revolting that they (the kids) will go to any extreme to flee their homes. Nowadays kids ride their bikes to cruise the malls, eat three-hour meals at fast food joints, or jab tweets into cell phones. To avoid parental glares, kids forsake their own rooms, fancy TVs, and a stocked refrigerator to seek the clamor of public places.

Dave and I had no such problems, because our parents rarely glanced at us, much less spoke. Also, we lacked the magnesium mountain bikes and supersonic skateboards of today's mobile youth.

As a consequence, we spent most of our time at home.

Yet, on thinking about it, that's not quite correct; we spent most of our time in Dave's backyard: digging, building villages, playing Army, and pursuing other boyish activities. We divided the balance of our days rather evenly between the two houses. Having grown up in mine, I find nothing worthy of note there. Dave's house, on the other hand, has earned a few comments.

Dave officially named his mother's house "The Bog" some years after he moved out. Not that it wasn't a bog when we frequented it as kids; we just didn't know the word. The term is just the most perfect description of the phenomenon Dave called *home*. As those blind from birth have no concept of color, Dave and I had no realization of the house's astonishing condition. When his horizons broadened in his late teens, Dave understood what he saw and uttered, "My God, a bog!"

Items set upon a bog will sit a moment, quiver, and then sink from view. So it was in Dave's house. Like a bog, thick gray-brown dust swallowed everything. Even the shapes of large objects became vague and amorphous submerged in the bountiful deposits. The living room in particular had been abandoned to the encroaching silt. All the chairs were piled high with old newspapers, boxes, or clothing. Obstructions choked the floor, leaving just a narrow tortuous path from the kitchen to the back bedrooms. If archeologists were to employ carbon dating, I'd predict the grime that coated the bookcases predated King Tut by a generous margin.

I recall a bright summer's day when a sunbeam had struggled through a mottled window and cast itself upon the living room floor (a sunbeam being the only thing that wouldn't sink). As Dave led the way to his room, he breezed along the path, and his tall, slender body drew a dust vortex up behind him. The sight reminded me of a jet plane landing on a humid morning.

How beautiful it was, glittering in the sunbeam resembling specks of gold! It swirled, and sparkled, then settled, sinking back into the bog. A bold epiphany struck me as I realized that, in Dave's house, the debris conquered everything—pervasive and unconquerable.

While Polly, Dave's mother, had abandoned

the living room to the encroaching elements, she worked hard in her knitting shop she'd stuffed into the converted garage. One of Polly's talents was dress design, along with knitting and the social discourse that accompanies both. Her shop became a natural gathering place for her lady friends. It was comparatively dust-free, although in retrospect, I'd guess her clients dusted the place as they moved about the crowded aisles in full dresses. But nature abhors a vacuum, so if the dust had given up, skeins of yarn rushed in with a vengeance. Thousands of skeins of every imaginable color jammed the shelves and hunkered under the chairs. They smothered the tables, oozed through the door toward the kitchen, and covered the floor so completely I'm not sure if it was carpeted or tiled. Yet, when I close my eyes to imagine Polly's shop, it wasn't full of yarn, but of laughter and chatter.

It takes courage to recreate the kitchen, even in the mind. While I'm sure Dave and I invaded the refrigerator from time to time, my mental self-defenses will not permit me to conjure the image. I never saw the sink, as it was buried under what I believe were dishes. Like the mountains they resembled, the dishes never moved. Never. The roaches did—but slowly because sheer gluttony gave them Sumo-like waist sizes. I never asked Polly, but it's not beyond the realm of possibility that the roaches had names. For fifteen years I visited the house every day and never saw a meal prepared. Now, decades later, Dave remains slender. Old habits die hard.

Because the passage from boyhood to manhood mandates rebellion against parents, Dave's room was an oasis of neatness in stark contrast to the rest of the house. He made his bed (on most days) and set his toys in precise rows on the shelves. I remember the small room being dark, which made it cozy and intimate, not dank as a dungeon might be. We didn't play in his room; it was too small. But he kept wooden chests and cardboard cartons of toys there, so we'd visit often, stock up with the day's props, and go to our shack in the backyard. There, we'd pursue our fantasies in the midst of our own western town built from discarded crates from Dick's shop.

But that's another tale.

In many ways, it's sad to think of Dave's father. He seemed to spend a large part of his life in misery. Even as a kid, I knew of his agony; my parents often spoke of it, nodding knowingly. The dilemma was simple: Dick, a devout Catholic, had married a divorced woman—a mortal sin—which drove him to drink and loneliness. Yet what could he do? His wife was gifted and warm. Her laughter, tinkling like carriage bells, drew him into her orbit. Dick hungered for her, and in retribution God banished him to the everlasting fires.

Although Dick was sullen, he doled out sporadic fits of generosity. While my own father was remote and ethereal, Dave's father was earthy and warm and I felt no fear of him, even though he'd bellow and swear at the smallest infraction. Dave, on the other hand, was often beaten by his father and moved warily in his presence.

Dick's domain was his shop. I'd guess it was about twenty by forty feet long and crouched behind the main house. It was constructed of white wooden siding and ill-fitting windows made myopic by ancient spider web cataracts. A hulking table saw, a wood lathe, and a giraffe-like band saw squatted in wood shavings and sawdust. Glue clamps, cans of varnish, and honed chisels peeked from half-open drawers lit by flickering fluorescent shop-lights. The room had never seen a vacuum cleaner or broom.

Dick loved the band saw. He'd often cut muskets and dueling pistols from planks of paper crates for Dave and me. With clever strokes of paint, he transformed the wooden weaponry into credible looking arms. On the lathe, he'd turn delicate bowls by the dozen—delicate, thin-walled and sanded to a high sheen. Dave's house was filled with bowels, and they in turn, were filled with junk. Dozens of bowls never escaped the shop and were scattered everywhere among the empty jugs of Gallo wine.

Although I'm sure he made clandestine forays into the house (Dave had a younger brother and sister), Dick spent virtually all his time, waking and sleeping, in his shop.

In the early fifties, I remember Dick taking a succession of jobs as a pressman. He often encountered philosophical differences with management and quit. Retaliating against the world of regimen and bosses, he bought a small printing press and began his own business in the shop. The first press, a small Kluge (a *snapper*, he called it), was soon paired with a larger one. The clutter became augmented by a good-sized paper cutter, a type tray reminiscent of Benjamin Franklin, hundreds of ink cans, and tons of unruly piles of paper. And gallon jugs of Gallo Muscatel.

The Catholic Church and the local Ford dealer became steady customers. By the time I graduated from high school in 1957, technology compelled him to buy an offset press, which he hated as a bastard born of compromise between quality and economics.

There is an aroma in a print shop that causes a nasal double take. The inks and cleaning solvent mingle together creating an odor of historical significance, a scent dating back hundreds of years. In Dick's shop, this smell blended with the fragrance of cedar shavings and Muscatel into a truly unique *nose,* as the vintners call it. I've been to print shops since then, and they smell sterile by comparison. Later, when divorce struck Dick and Polly, he moved to another place and took the fragrance with him.

In his middle age, Dick seemed to find solace in wine, and I'm convinced it killed him. He died in his late fifties as he had lived—lonely and angry, yet possessed of a touch of magic.

To make room for a modern apartment building, contractors torn down the shop along with Dave's house. But just the wood is gone, and when I close my eyes, a vivid image appears. I can see the balding and a somewhat overweight man sawing a musket from scrap wood or melting lead printer's type to cast "Pirate" coins for Dave and me. I can hear him say "bon far" when he spoke of making a bonfire. I can hear the squeal of the band saw and the clatter of the Kluge. I savor the aromatic cedar whirling from the lathe. I recall the pride I felt when Dick let me feed business cards into the snapper (set to run very slowly, of course). Even now, I remember the sense of wealth when he gave us a dozen empty one-gallon wine bottles to take to the paint store to exchange for a nickel apiece. Dave and I would save the jugs until we'd have two wagonloads—enough to buy a few pounds of chicken feed.

But that's another story.

Children and animals walk hand in hand. Even though American Indians often venerated their kinship with animals with totems, kids don't need wooden carvings. They just treasure their furry comrades (or *feathered*, in this case).

The setting for this tale is "The Cathouse", not to be confused with dens of sin, but considered literally—a house for felines. Before my parents bought our house in 1946, it belonged to the conductor of the Huntington Park Symphony Orchestra and his wife. He had a passion for

Zerbo Health Remover

concrete and she for cats. He'd built a miniature golf course in the backyard, and she had a wooden cathouse for tens of cats. In the end, it harbored trashcans for my father. But many years ago, it served a far nobler role.

I must have been about ten when I saw a dead bird in the street. I'd seen others before, but in my rush toward maturity, I'd never *seen* them. That day I did! The sparrow was on its back, spread-eagled in the street. Its beak gaped, and ants crawled in and out of its eye sockets while the downy feathers of its belly waved gently in the breeze. Patty and Joy, neighbor kids up the street, stood beside me and stared at the stomach-churning sight. Somber, we found a shoebox, wrapped the remains in my mother's finest tissue, and plopped it in a shallow hollow we'd dug in an abandoned part of the miniature golf course. We all joined hands and administered the final rights.

Hunkering in the shade of an immense pepper tree in the front yard, we dwelt on the meaning of life. While kids' pain augers far deeper than adults', they rebound more quickly. Like the metamorphosis of an ugly caterpillar, their anguish often leads to new adventures. Hence, we rejected the bird's death and decided to correct the situation. What was needed was a bird hospital—a fine, modern hospital where the creature could have received proper care. It didn't matter that we lacked experience as veterinarians or hospital administrators; we were resolved (and that is the path to greatness and glory).

We commandeered the cathouse. Being only ten, headroom was ample, and though it lacked electricity (cats can see in the dark), the lone window gave enough light for a proper operating theater. When we yanked open the creaking door, we were greeted by filth: cobwebs, vermin of all kinds and, not dust, but dirt. No matter! Shovels first, then brooms, and finally a thorough hosing with water. Darkness halted our efforts, but I fell into bed that night knowing the morrow would bring salvation to the feathered ones.

The next morning, I burst into the sweet morning air and ran to the hospital, only to find Patty already there, wrinkling her button nose. "Stinks," she said, rubbing the toe of her shoe on an ankle.

My next breath confirmed her observation. Mildew. Big time. Old wood, long buried in clinging ivy, is a haven for odorous fungi. We stepped in to see if we'd become immune to the reek, but teary eyes and burning throats drove us away.

Joy ambled up and coughed. "What in the world did you do? It smells like garbage."

Patty, being chatty that morning, uttered the solution, "Paint."

Kids and paint—a match made in heaven. We liberated leftover cans from my father's garage, mixed them together, and painted everything except the floor. The resulting glow was wonderful—just like a real hospital. But the stench of the drying paint (oil base in those days) banished us for the rest of the day.

The next morning we returned with a table (wobbly leg), a stool, a basket for the sick, clean rags, and a pilfered can of Band-Aids. (Yes, back in the fifties they came in metal cans.) We completed our surgical supplies with Listerine disinfectant, a small bottle of Mercurochrome pilfered from my Boy Scout first-aid kit, and a flashlight.

Joy folded the rags neatly, and Pattie brushed aside a dust speck as we continued our critical inspection. A nod from each and we declared the hospital open for business.

The only thing lacking were patients, so we set out to find ailing birds. There were none in my yard, nor in Missa Van's, nor over by Tosties. None up the street past Joy's or even Patty's. There were none on the next street by Tante's and none on Cherokee Road. We walked and walked and words became few. The shadows grew long and so did our faces. No sick birds. I began to wish God would break one of their wings so we could show our stuff. Patty spotted a limping dog, but even with only three legs, he escaped our lunges.

Night fell on our empty hospital.

Kids have little patience, and the hospital closed the next morning. Not that we said it was closed, or even that we returned the Band-Aids. It simply didn't enter our minds. No matter. Future adventures would have the cathouse become a prison and a warehouse.

But that's another tale or two.

The Warehouse

Young boys often seek fanciful places that capture their imaginations and sweep them away into worlds of adventure. Kids' shrines needn't be elaborate like the Taj Mahal, the Vatican, or the Mayan pyramids. For me, one of those magical places was the cathouse.

In my father's backyard, wearing a cloak of dense ivy, stood a fine shed, once home to a swarm of cats. It was dank and dark, the way I imagine the Amazon jungle must be. At one time it had been painted dark green—the perfect camouflage that hid the shed in smothering foliage. Its creaking door swung perilously on worn hinges, and a lone grimy window admitted feeble light. The roof was tall in front, but sloped so low at the far end that even kids had to stoop. It abutted a large lath house that nestled between the weed-ridden croquet court and the dilapidated miniature golf course.

Young boys can be meaner than cobras or rabid dogs and harbor an intense disdain for girls. Several such female creatures resided on my block, but one in particular was a garrulous, know-it-all threat to male superiority. Her name was Joy (a misnomer for sure). I decided she deserved to be put in her place, to be fed a gallon of humble and to have the perennial smirk wiped from her face. Unencumbered by ethics, Dave and I came up with a solution after discussing many options. We locked her up in the cathouse and renamed the place "The Downey Jail."

We scurried away shaking with laughter, savoring Joy's shrieks.

But we weren't the only ones who heard her bellowing. Mother did, too. In seconds, Joy was liberated, and I was grounded. When my father got home that night, we had a "discussion" involving his belt. I guess he obliterated *my* smirk.

A year or two later, Joy and I had come to terms, and with her friend Patty, we converted the jail to a bird hospital. For lack of patients, it lasted only a day and languished in disuse for months.

But when Dave and I became hardened businessmen at age twelve or so, the hospital assumed a new role. We'd begun raising chickens and needed money for feed. The local paint store paid cash for glass bottles to fill with paint thinner. (Today, OSHA would shut them down and stuff lawyer's bank accounts with cash.) To our parents' dismay, every trash day Dave and I rummaged through the neighbor's trashcans salvaging bottles. Once our Radio Flyer wagons overflowed, we'd haul the booty back to the shed for storage. That's when the hospital became the warehouse.

There was a further aid to our fundraising. Dave's father enjoyed a nip of wine from time to time, and empty Gallo gallon jugs accumulated at an amazing rate, adding to our good fortune. Somehow, we acquired large wood trays from the Helms Bakery (damaged I'm sure) and filled them with glass treasures.

When the bottles overflowed the warehouse, Dave and I made a pilgrimage to the paint store. We'd lash crates of bottles on our wagons as high as our eyes and tie them to our bikes train-fashion. With red faces, we'd strain on the pedals and tow the teetering, clattering load downtown.

As our chicken business grew, the warehouse also housed sacks of feed, straw bales, and other avian paraphernalia. For several years it was our industrial hub until Dave and I trekked from the realm of childhood into adolescence. High school and a deadly chicken disease ended our poultry venture. Without a need for feed or bottles, the warehouse once more reverted to a mere shed.

Decades later, I look back and mourn the tawdry demise of the warehouse. My thoughts give way to recollections of glorious adventures and how the shed evolved from a cathouse to jail to hospital to warehouse. In truth, it wasn't any of these things—it was a pillar supporting an emerging life—a youngster reaching for adulthood.

With vivid memories nestled on my lap, I smile and nod in homage to the lowly shed that became a magical place that nudged me toward maturity.

Zerbo Health
Remover

Zerbo began as one of those idle summer-day
larks when Dave and I had exhausted all the
usual play alternatives such as Big Army or Mining
Camp. We were around ten years old at the time,
and as boredom set in, we naturally gravitated

to the kitchen. It must have been Dave's kitchen because we were never allowed to tamper in mine.

A word or two might be in order about our respective kitchens: they were, of course, not ours but our parents'. Dave's mother, Polly, never noticed two small urchins prowling in her domain, but my mother was the Grand Inquisitor. "What are you boys into now?" she'd query. In contrast, Polly orbited in her own extraterrestrial world of her yarn shop she'd set up, so we played mostly at Dave's.

As normal growing boys are, the afternoon's idleness settled in our stomachs, and we wandered into Polly's kitchen. The counter top hadn't been seen for months, buried in ancient dishes by day and smothered by roaches at night. Corroded forks. Crusted plates. Ossified slabs of bread. Glasses stratified with brown liquid in the bottom and a layer of green semi-solid covering the top. Nothing edible in sight, and we weren't particular!

We sauntered from fridge to drawer to cabinet searching for a bite. As the spice cabinet came under scrutiny, a tiny spark of kid-magic flashed. We didn't say anything; it just happened. First, there was a small gleam in our eyes as we achieved that Buddha-like state where we communicated without words. Then, stifled giggles were followed by gleeful plans as we came to the glorious realization that a divinely-inspired revelation had unfolded.

We forgot our empty stomachs and embraced

our new adventure. It began in a saucepan with a half pint of vinegar and grew as we added every spice imaginable. Then we tossed in hot peppers followed by food coloring, tomato paste, gobs of garlic, baking soda, and a very interesting unidentifiable liquid from the fridge. The brew radiated various iridescent shades as it settled and required vigorous stirring to stay mixed. It was truly a vile concoction that tasted as horrid as it looked. (Yes, we actually sampled the vat as we formulated it!)

Such a magnificent creation demanded a suitable container, so we crept into the bathroom, unearthed a jug of cough syrup, and emptied it down the sink. The bottle was one of those long obsolete apothecary items, having scientific cubic centimeter graduations along the side. Perfect! Putting on our official angelic demeanors, Dave and I approached Polly and supplicated ourselves. "You got any labels?" we asked. We knew that was a perfectly stupid question—Polly *always* had everything. She produced a grand looking gummed label on which we painstakingly lettered **ZERBO HEALTH REMOVER**. With the precision of a brain surgeon, we gave our elixir a final stir and filled the bottle. With a nod, we shook hands. "Better than vintage wine," Dave pronounced.

As an adult, I have sought the glory I felt at that moment. To our unfettered brains, our creation surpassed the invention of television. Zerbo, silly as it seems, reigns in my childhood reminiscences as a flawless afternoon filled with laughter.

An epilogue: the next day, Dave and I made the rounds of the neighborhood attempting to sell swigs of Zerbo. We didn't expect to succeed, of course, but visions of grumpy adults swooning in agony, and gasping for air kept us trying. These same grownups would see us often as we peddled corncob pipes, plaster broaches, or sailing boats fashioned from walnut shells.

But that's another story.

The Merchants of Downey

In keeping with the fine traditions of the Silk Road, the Santa Fe Trail and Interstate 70, modern society is driven to trade goods. So it is with young boys (two of them, anyway). Moreover, merchants need worthy products to sell, and manufacturing is a talent that young boys also possess (two of them, anyway).

Vivid imagination resides in dark corners of kids' minds and can make the silliest object a candidate for greatness. Dave and I discovered that a walnut shell is such an item. Adults smash them and wantonly dig out the meat. Boys, however, see opportunity lurking in everything, even walnuts. We were no exception.

If a walnut is carefully split and its contents surgically extracted, two beguiling half-shells remain. Dave noted that one end resembled the prow of a tiny ship.

"What we have," he said, "is a miniature canoe or one of those hide-covered boats the Indians used to make."

"So?" I said, unimpressed.

"We can sell them—make big money."

"Come on. Who'd want to buy half a walnut shell?"

Dave stood, jammed his hands into his pockets and frowned. "That's a point. We need to fix it up—make it cool."

An hour later we'd transformed the simple bullboat of the Lewis and Clark era into an elegant sailing vessel. A toothpick anchored in candle wax served as a mast. A small square of paper became the mains'l and a dab of modeling clay served as a cradle.

After we'd built half a dozen ships, Dave announced, "We're in business."

I set the fragile items in a discarded cigar box and we sallied forth to the neighbors, hawking the ships to whoever answered the door. Only the elderly Missa Van graced our palms with a dime, the going price for our elegant collectable.

That night, scowls of frustration covered our faces as we tried to understand the meager revenues.

"I don't get it," Dave muttered. "Our ships are cool. Even the price is right."

"Maybe they don't think we're serious businessmen."

Dave furrowed his brows. "You know? JC Penney has hundreds of customers. Why? They sell gobs of different things, but we have just one. We need more stuff."

"Makes sense."

For over an hour, we pondered, quibbled, and weighed many ideas but couldn't come up with a breakthrough product. It was Dave's mother who inspired a grand solution.

"I made this when I was in grade school," she said, showing us a broach.

Young boys and broaches are on different planets, so Dave and I were not exactly thrilled.

"I sold dozens at the church bazaar."

That got our attention.

"They're easy to make," she said. "Clip a small picture of a flower or any fun thing from a magazine, wet it, and paste it face down in a spoon. Then, fill the spoon with plaster of Paris and stick in a safety pin. When it dries, the broach pops out real easy."

Visions of vast riches, cute girls fawning in

adoration, and limitless ice cream spiraled in my head. Dave, wordless for once, just grinned.

The next day after school, Dave and I converted his kitchen into a broach factory. Glossy magazines, looking moth-eaten from our scissors, were scattered on the floor. Semi-hardened plaster caked the lip of a saucepan while we arrayed a dozen plaster-filled spoons in neat rows. I was confident that Henry Ford would have been proud of our production line.

The following afternoon, Dave and I made the rounds in our neighborhood. Dave's mother was right; we sold several broaches, even another sailing ship. I felt like the chairman of General Motors.

Emboldened by success, Dave and I expanded our line again. The next stroke of genius was corncob pipes. We scavenged cobs from the dinner table and tossed them to the scrawny chickens that roamed Dave's backyard. Within a few days, the birds picked them clean, and the sun dried them out. It was easy to sand the cob, hollow its inside and insert a bamboo stem. We weren't chummy with General MacArthur, but I'm sure he would have purchased a pipe.

With three products, our undertaking felt like a massive conglomerate, except the corporate officers wore jeans, T-shirts and tennies, not power suits. As upcoming entrepreneurs, we needed a name for our company, so we combined portions of our last names and dubbed the firm Gunons Enterprises. The future was ours.

But economic reality struck. Dave and I learned that the market is a fickle thing; the neighbors grew tired of two grubby kids peddling tacky curios. We tried selling on distant streets, but strange urchins are irritants, not cute, and sales totaled zero.

Newton's fifth law states that resilient young boys are never vanquished and our quantum leap arrived soon—chickens.

Chickens? True enough, but that's another tale.

ROCKET MAN

Sooner or later all young boys develop a fascination for things that *go bang*. Because I was a semi-normal kid, I was determined to set fire to the neighborhood and developed an interest in rockets. Soon, it was more than interest; it became an obsession.

The first symptoms were innocent enough: a few books on rockets and space travel, soon accompanied by a genuine propulsion textbook. To squelch the tedium of civics class, I memorized the equation for mass ratios of multi-stage rockets and wrote it reverently over and over and over while the teacher droned away. Somehow, I passed civics.

Youngsters, of course, have heroes. So did I. Not Yogi Berra or Elvis, but Robert Goddard and Werner von Braun. My friends thought I was dorky—a trait I considered satisfying. Even today, decades later, I prefer to think of myself as an oddball.

But one does not attain greatness by reading convoluted books or worshiping heroes. So, in a quest for glory, I put my inspirations to the test and launched a succession of pyrotechnic adventures.

My initial attempts were rudimentary. I'd wrap foil around a match head and hold a candle under it until it "cooked off." The match, hissing and sputtering, leapt perhaps a few feet. After two or three trials, I succumbed to boredom and, to the horror of my parents, began launching model rockets I purchased at the hobby shop.

Now I was onto something! Like a king, I'd strut to the center of the park and set up my launching platform. A group of curious youngsters would gather around, making me feel like hot stuff—particularly if there was a cute girl in the crowd. I'd make my preparations with the dramatic flourishes of a concert pianist and bark sage pronouncements like a college professor.

At T-minus ten, I'd wave the crowd back, warning that rockets were extremely dangerous. When satisfied that all was in order, I'd solemnly chant, "Five, four, three, two, one, launch!"

The thing took off like, well—a rocket! The cheers of the kids made my chest puff out, nearly popping the buttons from my shirt. Hot stuff for sure!

I guess the Rocket God disapproved of my grandiose conceit and ordained stern justice. One day, I launched my pride and joy on a windy afternoon, and at its apogee, the parachute deployed and carried my rocket far downwind. I never found it. I figured it landed two states away—maybe in Montana.

Humbled, I decided that toy missiles were for

children, not high school gurus, and embarked on serious science: designing rocket engines. Not silly match heads, solid-fuel ones or hobby store offerings, but liquid fueled imitations of von Braun's V-2s.

First, I tried to build a rocket motor in an Erlenmeyer flask pilfered from my chemistry set. No luck; I couldn't get it to belch, much less thunder as an honest rocket would.

Then, I snatched a fifty-seven-millimeter shell casing (I've no idea where it came from) and lashed it to a heavy workbench. I drilled holes for fuel injectors and nailed a scientific looking plywood blast shield in place. I salvaged faucets from a discarded sink to serve as fuel control valves. While searching for fuel tanks, gasoline, and hydrogen peroxide to power my creation, my father suggested that I find another recreation (I'm being euphemistic).

No matter that the authorities canceled my project; glory goes to the persistent! It was easy to capitalize on talents gained in my sophomore drafting class. I took up my textbook on rocket engine design and waded into mind-bending conjuring. Squinting over a crude drawing board, I whipped up drawings for the world's most exotic rocket engine with recirculating cooling, a proper nozzle, and innovative fuel injectors. I was certain my design would set the scientific world on its ear! Hot stuff!

But real rocket engineers don't lounge at

the beach when their fancy drawings are done; they're driven to prove their mettle on the field of battle. So I decided to build and test my creation. My father slapped his forehead at the news, but mother helped me name the critter: *Phlogiston*, the ancient element of fire.

With money from my paper route, I contracted with a foundry to have castings poured, and purchased a used metal lathe (Sears Roebuck) to machine the parts. With contempt, I shoved my father's tools aside and erected a magnificent rocket factory in the garage. Cape Canaveral must have been jealous. Hot stuff!

But as I eased further into my senior year, the quest for adulthood scuttled my rocket journey. Unfinished rocket parts turned orange with rust and the lathe sank into the dust, a surefire treasure for a future archeologist.

In the late sixties, I went on to test *real* rocket engines, ones that actually went into space. Today, decades later, I'm unsure what became of the lathe and castings, but I still have the rusty fuel injectors and engineering drawings.

Do I continue to design rocket engines or launch projectiles at the moon? Nope. I've moved on to things such as house payments, children, and a career in engineering, but I know one thing for sure—memories are hot stuff!

Overnight with Tante

Gladys was my mother's sister and, being ten years older, always seemed ancient. I never knew my maternal grandmother who died when I was six or seven. My paternal grandmother stayed twenty miles away with another aunt, so I didn't see much of her. But Tante, as we called Aunt Gladys, lived close by and often coddled my brother Mark and me with fervor. In a way, I've always thought of her as my grandmother, and she doted on me as if she were. My mother always said that Tante was a gorgeous young woman and very popular with the gentlemen. But she was a free spirit and never found a beau suitable for the long haul. So

Tante became the traditional "Old Maid" grade school teacher. Mother, wielding her racy sense of humor, would leer and say, "She'll die wondering."

But make no mistake; Tante was never traditional! As an elementary school teacher, she taught first, second, or third grade in a series of schools. I'm certain she was a good teacher because she had a passion about her charges but couldn't abide paperwork and yard duty. She simply declined to do either. School administrators tolerated her eccentricities for a year or two and then canned her. I'm not sure if she ever got tenure. Like a nomad following antelope migrations, Tante trekked from school district to school district leaving behind inspired children and confused administrators.

When I was in second or third grade, Tante landed a job at the local elementary school where I attended. She took a small cottage behind one of the nicer, if older, houses just a few blocks away. Occasionally my parents allowed me to spend the night with her.

Now, decades later, I can't describe the cottage, give you its floor plan or color scheme. But I remember it smacked of Victorian elegance, and a quiet regal aura bathed everything in its glow. The house seemed large and airy, and I felt warm and secure there. The decor included mahogany-framed photos of my grandparents, delicate doilies, and fluffy comforters. There wasn't a single masculine stroke in the room, which figured, I suppose.

Tante set a simple table with a single candle or perhaps a small bouquet plucked from the garden. She served wholesome fare, and the entire meal was filled with her admonitions, "Eat a bit more. Try the peas. Want more Jell-O?" I remember getting agitated because she treated me like a baby! Much later, when I was in my fifties, I had a meal with her, and she said, "Eat a bit more. Try the peas. Want more Jell-O?" Some things never change.

After dinner, she'd read from a big yellow children's book, or maybe we'd play Parcheesi. I'd get antsy from inactivity, and she'd scold me in a sharp voice. But seconds later she'd be her usual self, which could only be described as syrupy.

Tante was the consummate armchair traveler, and her passion was Paris. Fear of flying and a modest budget diverted her attention to dozens of books that touted the glories of the Eiffel Tower and the Musée d'Orsay. Not a casual faux Parisian, she memorized the street maps of the city and embraced the masters of impressionist art: Monet, Degas, and even Gauguin.

Oddly enough, I welcomed bedtime. I think her spare bed was a double because it seemed immense to my young perspective. It had a puffy flowered comforter that I'd tug over my ears in cozy pleasure. To this day I still draw my blankets over my ears to sleep.

Thinking about it now, maybe Tante was a little shrewder than she looked, because bedtime began with a treat: a few minutes of music from her record player. She had two musical passions: Dixieland jazz and Bing Crosby. Bing crooned a song called *Far Away Places* that in quiet moments still floods my head decades later. (I'm forced by history to apply the verb *croon* to Bing's singing.) I remember lying there in the warm yellow light of the cottage listening to Bing warble, "Those far away places, with the strange sounding names." Even the lyrics are engraved in my mind.

We'd listen to Dixie too, although I can't recall any specific tunes. During those visits, Tante seeded Dixieland jazz into my nearly vacant young skull where it blossomed. It strikes me as odd that Elvis' assault on my generation, the Beatles, and the other rock and rollers never touched me the way her Dixie did. To this day I revel in it. I can close my eyes and drift back to those years. Bubbling clarinets and rattling pianos swirled around the cottage as I drifted into the land of nod—warm, wanted, with the comforter pulled over my ears.

An Old Man's Lament

While this account of my childhood adventures may shine a light on the blossoming of a child into an adult, cute anecdotes aren't the whole story. Everyone has cherished snapshots of their youth that makes past moments vivid, such as kids huddling inside a makeshift bedroom tent on a rainy day. Perhaps a jolt from the past brings an ancient soccer goal to life, or accolades for an "A" on a nearly forgotten English test.

Mirth grips me when I recall the night my father sat at the dining table, and lurched crazily as the chair leg broke through a termite-ridden floor.

Or when the plaster on the kitchen ceiling fell into my mother's meatloaf.

Or when the five immense peppertrees fell into decay one by one, making my yard feel naked.

Or when my father staggered out the door in the middle of the night as my mother writhed in labor with my sister-to-be. He frantically tried to zip his fly, but he'd put his pants on backwards.

I suppose he checked mom into the hospital with his ass hanging out.

Gone is the huge bush where I made a fort to play hide and seek.

Gone are the croquet court, the cathouse, the fishpond, and the twin palm trees in the front yard.

Gone are Dave's house, Dick's shop, and the shack—all demolished to make room for a sterile, ugly apartment building.

My childhood world was erased when my home, and the miniature golf course were bulldozed for two new modern houses.

Today, Dave's wolf-call still echoes in canyons of fresh stucco, but there are no ears to hear it.

All this happened while I was away making my own adult life, and I paid no mind. Only in old age do I yearn for the reek of acid, and the sight of skid marks on the sidewalk. Once taken for granted, the smell of roasting marshmallows over a pot-bellied stove is precious to me now.

I guess we're all like that in some way. My memories were created in Downey, California, but others were born in Boston, Biloxi or Barcelona. Grownups everywhere may be reading a book or watching TV and suddenly pause as a childhood memory flashes before their eyes—a tear, a sniffle, and then a grin.

No matter. Everyone has one thing in common— we were all kids once.

THE END

Printed in the United States
By Bookmasters